teresa wilms montt

IN THE STILLNESS
OF MARBLE

with a preface by
enrique gómez carrillo

translated and with an afterword by
jessica sequeira

THIS IS A SNUGGLY BOOK

Translation and Afterword Copyright © 2019
by Jessica Sequeira.
All rights reserved.

ISBN: 978-1-943813-82-7

IN THE STILLNESS OF MARBLE

TERESA WILMS MONTT was born on September 8, 1893 in Viña del Mar, Chile, into an elite, well-connected family. Her first book, *Inquietudes sentimentales*, consisted of fifty poems with surrealist features, while her second, *Los tres cantos*, explored eroticism and spirituality. Both books enjoyed great success in Argentine intellectual circles. In 1918, she moved to Madrid, where she published two works widely recognized by Spanish literary critics: *In the Stillness of Marble* and *Anuarí*. Upon returning to Buenos Aires in 1919, she published her fifth book, *Cuentos para hombres que todavía son niños*. She died in 1921, in Paris, from an overdose of Veronal.

JESSICA SEQUEIRA was born in San Jose, California in 1989, and currently lives in Santiago de Chile. Her works include the novel *A Furious Oyster* (Dostoyevsky Wannabe), and the collection of essays *Other Paradises: Poetic Approaches to Thinking in a Technological Age* (Zero). Her translations include Adolfo Couve's *When I Think of My Missing Head* (Snuggly) and Liliana Colanzi's *Our Dead World* (Dalkey Archive).

Contents

Preface: Thérèse de la Cruz / *7*

Introduction / *13*
Offering / *15*

For Anuarí / *17*
Oh! now I cannot write your name / *18*
In a letter / *20*
Lie quietly, Anuarí / *22*
Anuarí; I evoke you / *23*
I draw your gaze / *25*
In the darkness of my thoughts / *26*
Since you left / *28*
With my head reclined / *30*
The hours fall / *32*
The curtains move / *34*
As usual, today I went to see you / *35*

At night, I enter my bedroom / *37*
I find a certain relief / *39*
I am ill / *42*
Anuarí . . . / *44*
Anuarí, my darling / *46*
Anuarí; my sweet precious one / *48*
I woke up with a start / *50*
With a sleepwalker's step / *53*
Anuarí, Anuarí! / *55*
Anuarí, men would judge me crazy / *56*
Like the souls that inhabit the cloisters / *58*
Wandering through lonely forests / *60*
Today I brought jasmines / *61*
The ice that melts / *63*
Before my eyes / *65*
Alone, amidst my papers and books / *67*
I have turned off all the lights / *69*
Anuarí, I look at my lips / *71*
You came to me / *73*
My life is yours / *74*
Anuarí, Anuarí, why did you go? / *75*
I move away . . . / *77*
Anuarí, goodbye for now / *79*

Afterword: Writing to the Dead / *81*

Thérèse de la †

Those who see her pass, slender and rhythmic, with her 'locks' cut short and her insolent little walking stick, wonder if she is a Russian ballerina, or a fantastical Parisian, or a North American millionaire who for eyes has bought the two biggest and most pure emeralds in the world.

To tell the truth, I do not know exactly where she is from. But I know that she is definitely not from here, that she comes from a time before seas, before skies, before human races, maybe even before souls existed, and that like one of Maeterlinck's characters, she seems to be looking for a crown in the depths of a miraculous fountain of gold and mist.

Teresa! . . . or Thérèse? . . . de la Cruz! . . . And without her thinking about it, without her wanting it, behind her cross lies the devil. There he is for us poor sensitive men, the evil companion of Saint Anthony, with all his temptations and flattery. But she knows how to say to those who approach her asking for alms from her lips: 'What, but we're *compañeros!*'

And it's true . . . This woman who bears the burden of the curse of her beauty is not only a writer, a great writer who if she were a man and had a beard would form part of all the Academies and wear all the medals.

It's only that, yes, she is a woman, and the most lovely of women! Who has not been in love with her? . . . Who has not felt before her adolescent wolf's mouth the terrible emotion of the infinite? . . . Who has not offered his entire soul in exchange for a smile? . . .

She has always answered:

'Ah . . .'

Only one day, before two crazed eyes in the face of a martyr, did her pale, very pale emeralds perhaps moisten. But then, shaking her mane of a young lioness, she had the heroism to open her heart and reveal herself to a corpse . . .

Because this brilliant mad girl, who goes through existence scattering the white pearls of her smile, is a poor tormented thing who suffers more for someone that does not exist than for those dying on her behalf.

I say to her:

'You are not from here; you are from another town, another race; you cannot live except in the forest of a sleeping princess or a vault of kings; you are an idol for worshippers of a different species . . . Go from here; my God . . .'

She laughs with her laugh, which is that of a girl and a demon:

'Don't be crazy! . . .'

Who is the crazier of the two? . . . She, in any case, has genius as her excuse, which is a magnificent and fatal sign of madness. I possess nothing, nothing more than the two eyes of a martyr which wake the beloved dead.

Gómez Carillo
El Liberal, 18 May 1918.

IN THE STILLNESS OF MARBLE

Introduction

I do not want to suppress a single one of these lines, for that would be to kill their painful spontaneity, and to conceal the anguished torment suffered by the soul of the one who wrote them.

Offering

I lay at your feet the gentle offering of my book, which I place before them like the most delicate perfume of my inspiration.

Along the lengthy road that separates you from the sham of the place where you lie in the sublime and chaste stillness of marble, I have gone, shedding my soul of its miserable human ties; I have gone, purifying it with bloody martyrdoms to bring it to you, clarified like the water of a fountain not deflowered by the light of day.

Do not be afraid that my pages will leave an impure mark on your bed. Even if you have sublimated yourself in death, I have redeemed myself by losing my sheath of mud in an overwhelming whirlwind of pain.

You can accept my offering as gently as my flowers, since neither the one nor the other will disturb your sleep.

Accept it; I offer it to you with limpid eyes and a calm face, turned toward the world that must judge me, with my spirit light and useless like the smoke of an incense burner.

Thérèse Wilms.
Madrid 1918.

I

For Anuarí: who sleeps in this coffin of eternal sleep.

For him . . . my Anuarí, whom no one can now compete with me for; because my love, my love and pain, give me the right to possess him completely. Sleeping body and radiant soul.

Yes, Anuarí, this book is for you. Didn't you ask me for it one afternoon, your hands in mine, my eyes in your eyes, your mouth in my mouth, in intimate communion? and I, all soul, said to you: Yes—kissing you deeply in the middle of your heart.

Do you remember, Anuarí?

II

Oh! now I cannot write your name without a veil of tears hiding my eyes, and a tight knot strangling my throat.

'Why did you go, love? why?' I ask myself a thousand, two thousand times a day. And I am unable to find any reply that soothes the fierce pain of my soul.

Yes: why did you go, Anuarí, and not take me with you?

Looking at your portrait with the passion of a mother, a fiancée, a lover crazed with love, I try to wrench from your gaze the great enigma that has destroyed your life and mine.

Ah, my precious one! When cruel luck snatched those two daughters of my blood from me, I thought my pain had burst human limits. But no; you have made my desperate cry arrive at the throne of the Christian God himself, which it addresses trembling, with wild and sacred outrage.

One cannot be so cruel to a weak creature without giving her sufficient strength to bear the lashings, and abandoning her afterward in agony. Yes; your silent departure has left me near death on the edge of infinite nothingness; and alone, with a thirst for affection, a longing for sleep and rest, surrender at last . . .

III

In a letter, you once wrote to me:

> *Per l'amor che rimane*
> *e a la vita resiste* (and ours will endure,
> isn't that so Teresa?)
> *Nulla é più dolce e triste*
> *che le cosa lontane.*[1]

Yes, Anuarí, 'nulla é più dolce e triste che le cosa lontane'. And that is why you left.

That letter I have reread once again, and as always it gives me a hopeless impression, which I can only translate into sobs.

---

1 Whether Wilms Montt was aware of it or not, the lines are by Gabriele D'Annunzio and translate to: *For the love that remains and the life that endures, nothing is sweeter and sadder than far-off things.*

Your letters, your portraits, and the flowers now dead on your coffin are relics I cling to with unhealthy greed: they form my whole ideal, my whole life, and if I do not say my consolation, it is because this no longer exists for me.

I also keep two screws, which with hard and impious hands the undertakers drove into your casket, screws to be pounded into my brain on the day of my death; into my brain, where your profound and immovable image has been chiseled, just as the centuries have mined fissures into the frozen rocks.

Anuarí, Anuarí! If it were possible to resurrect you, I would give up even my consciousness; I would resign myself to living prostrate at your feet like a slave, with the sole satisfaction of looking at you, and hearing you laugh, with that silver cascade of laughter; aspiring to no reward but to feeling, just once, the kiss of your mouth on my forehead.

Anuarí, come back to life! Come back to the warm cradle of my arms, where I will sing to you, until I become a single note that encloses your name.

IV

Lie quietly, Anuarí. I will always be yours. I have made my body a temple, where I worship your kisses and your caresses with the deepest adoration.

I bear, pierced in me like a dagger, your smile; in the place where my eyes rest is that smile with teeth pressed tightly together, making your mouth a bloody cocoon full of gleaming white seeds.

Anuarí. Your smile is a destructive obsession that mutes all my laughter, your smile provokes in my mind the restlessness of a lightning flash at midnight. A mother-of-pearl poison, it trickles into my heart and paralyzes it.

V

Anuarí; I evoke you sleeping and imagine you asleep for eternity.

A shadow spreads gently over my soul, the divine shadow of your lashes, which formed the two wings of a velvety butterfly beneath your eyes.

Yes, Anuarí. One night, the happiest of my life, you fell asleep with your head on my shoulder, and so intimate was my tenderness that my breathing became music to cradle you.

You slept, my precious one, after having wrung out my brain and my heart with your lips avid for youth, like a bee lustful for nectar and perfume.

And those shadows of your lashes are curtains that hide the sunlight from me, and carry me in a confused vertigo toward your deep Land.

One night, the happiest, the only night of my life, you fell asleep with your head on my chest, and found there the delight of dream, and sought the eternal pillow.

VI

I draw your gaze from the depth of silence; I evoke your eyes . . . and shudder. Even glazed by death, on me they have the effect of a lightning bolt. Their power to fascinate has not perished.

They are two blue headlights that show me the magnificent irradiations of the Infinite; they are two stars of the first magnitude that look deeply upon my sorrows, perforating them and widening the void, until they open a gap infinite as a world.

Your adored eyes, once reflections of that gorgeous soul of yours, now live in my mind sustained by my own life, taking on brilliance through the endless spring of my tears.

Anuarí. Just as your eyes chained me to your life, now they drag me to your grave, inviting me with temptations of delirium. Your eyes are two magnets before an abyss. I feel a fierce attraction . . .

VII

In the darkness of my thoughts I see your image appear wrapped in the mystery of death, with the terrifying halo of an unknown beyond. I call to you, all my soul concentrated in you; I call to you and it seems to me that the shadows are ripped apart by your winged step, like that of a bird wounded in full flight.

When I understand that I will never see you again, a wave of anguish rises in my heart, engulfing my brain in a vertigo of catastrophe, an anguish over this slaughter of life's beauty.

You are so strong and noble, with your serene face and your forehead lifted toward the sky.

Anuarí. Sorrow does not drive one mad, sorrow does not kill; it continues to deepen into the soul like a leaden body, with an infinite trembling. Astonished, at night I listen to the echo of my voice, as it searches for you awaiting a reply. The black truth wounds me and fills me with rage. Perhaps your spirit has died too? No; no! How is it possible that such vigor, the energy of a star, goes to perish in eternal ice?

VIII

Since you left, my eyes and my ears have lain in wait for your image . . . your steps; they are inclined toward death in fervent expectation of resurrection.

And on the gray days when the frozen wind blows, with the eyes of the soul I see you emerge white from your white shroud, transfigured by the serene, blessed embrace of the earth.

And when the sun spills out diamonds upon the world, then I breathe in all the flowers, I see you in all the trees, and I possess you tumbling, intoxicated with love, on the lawns of fragrant grass.

And when the moon gives its humble blessing to men, I see you gigantic, silhouetted by the sharp edges of a lightning bolt; I see you enormous, confused with the immortal, scattering your indulgence over the world, soothing the desperation of so many suffering castaways; I breathe you in the atmosphere, I imagine you in the mystery, I extract you from nothingness.

It seems to me that the world was only made to help me evoke you, and the sun to serve me as a lantern over the rugged path.

IX

With my head reclined between my arms, in an eagerness to sleep, I repeat, like children do, a prayer: your name.

Yes, Anuarí, I'm sleepy, very sleepy; that same lethargic drowsiness disturbed your soul before closing your adored eyes forever.

Like a prayer, syllable by syllable my lips spell out your name, and my hands, grown weak, search in the warm nest of your hair to hide themselves and die.

Anuarí, Anuarí!

As from a boiling spring, complaints and pleas well up from my chest. All of them leave to vanish in chaos, perhaps without ever arriving to you.

It is horrible, and I do not understand how

my body does not succumb to the weight of such a harsh burden.

Life without you is a dismal thing, which I trail along like an ignoble rag.

X

The hours fall like droplets of lead over a wasteland; they go to meet you, and I stay; I stay, gloomy, taciturn, wrapped in black ennui, as in a chainmail of iron.

Two months ago today, my precious one, you went down to a stone cavern, and to bear you in my heart paralyzed even my desire to cry.

Two months already! Without dying I saw how they brought your coffin through the Cemetery gate; through that gate with its jaws of a jackal, which never opens for the souls that pass through it, asleep.

In those two months, you had no caress but the light shy touch of my flowers, my poor flowers that are my only proof of love, the blessed offering that trembling with sorrow my soul lays upon your corpse.

Two months. My hands, beggars for caresses, try to draw out a tenderness from your coffin; but the wood, miserly with the treasure it encloses, makes itself rigid like a being that has not suffered.

Nothing, my Anuarí! All that reaches the depths of your grave, very muffled, as from a distant pack of hounds, are the noises of the world, the confused to and fro of men, those easily moved shadows that do not know where they come from or where they are going, for they are afraid of finding out.

Two months ago today, you left. The clock throbs; its tick-tock stamps against my brain, destroying my thoughts with its mournful steps toward deceitful Eternity.

Two months, and now I do not suffer as a result of so much suffering.

XI

The curtains move and the light trembles. With full intensity I ask the night if it is you who gives life to those things.

Anuarí.

On my back in bed, I hear only the furious knocking of my heart inside my chest.

Everything that surrounds me is steeped in mystery. The furniture speaks amongst itself of tragic secrets; the doors complain of their ever-enigmatic thresholds, awaiting someone who never arrives; and the lamp seems to discern a mute desperation.

The portraits look at me with a heartrending expression of sorrow. Anuarí, Anuarí! Already I know that my cry is lost without echo in the impious abyss of nothingness, but in order not to succumb I must call to you, clinging to an illusion that does not exist.

XII

As usual, today I went to see you; it was your day, the day of all those eternally at rest. I covered your coffin with red carnations, and imagined that their fragrance would reach through the wooden boards, to make you shiver with tenderness.

With my head resting on the casket I thought deeply of you.

An Olympian serenity cloaked my soul in a white tunic, calming all its bitterness.

There was no desperation in my pain.

I understood, my love, that for me the great gate to the infinite was open wide, opened by your lofty hands.

I saw, too, that you possessed wings able to set off in sumptuous flight toward the meeting, and then I felt consoled.

Hidden in your casket is the key to the great gate: you keep it in your right hand. When the miserable struggle overwhelms me, I will go look for it. I will open your hand with the kiss of a mother who wakes her child, and lacing it in mine, we will march together toward the sun, in search of its nuptial blessing. We will go, immortal children of the light, in pursuit of the irradiation of stars to crown our transparent heads. We will march together, ecstatic, serene, glorious, like a single blue flame of the soul of the Creator, to the sound of magisterial choirs that will harmonize with Nature our queen.

We will glide through the limpid spaces, sublime with goodness, singing an eternal *resurrexit*.

Touching your coffin my face grows pale, and my eyes search for the great gate.

XIII

At night, I enter my bedroom as I would a temple, so fervently that my knees buckle. For there is your portrait, looking at me with that unlimited goodness of pardon.

I kiss the frozen glass, in the place where your mouth shows through, and delight in illuminating your eyes with the reflection of mine, shining with emotion. On your forehead I bring together my hands, and in a tragic tremor of the soul, I beg for your company, the heat of your protection near my bed; in fervent longing I beg for the mystery to stretch over me the shroud of silence.

My precious one, I speak with your portrait, scattering over it things childish and deep, as if they were flowers; I cry, I laugh, and feeling you in my arms, I sing to you as if you had been born of me.

And you are born of me; and for me and in me you live, because for everyone else you are dead.

From the most noble blood of my heart, I drew you out and joined you to my destiny forever.

XIV

I find a certain relief in the monotonous repetition of my grief, such as the madman finds in his incoherent words, his expressive exaltations.

I love you, Anuarí . . .

The warmth of your body has remained like a sleepless poison in my limbs, which writhe in spasmodic convulsions of delirium and clamor for the sharp absence of your body, your young flesh perfumed by spring.

My mouth is thirsty with lust. Yes, Anuarí. During contortions of the possessed, there escape from me the heartrending howls of my flesh and wounded heart; amidst the spasms of pleasure and pain, there bursts forth, between the sighs, your name.

Ah! I have remained eager for you; anxious for your kisses.

And before the attraction of your radiant spirit, I remained blind as if I were looking at the sun.

My lips, eager, half-open, await the nectar of your love. And the time passes, and your balm of snow does not heal my wounds of fire.

The day flaunted all the dazzling regalia of Spring...

An Olympian ray of light dressed the flowers in tunics of diamond.

Before such ironic splendor, my heart felt with greater force your august solitude, and despising pomp, it went to offer itself to you, so the gentle veils of its melancholy could protect you.

I came to your niche, to your narrow and wretched cavern, with the desire to turn myself to velvet, to bundle you up, to wrap you in myself, to give you an impression of love; so that you would not realize, my precious one, that all considered you to be a useless object.

I do not understand the heat that animates my life, when you are so rigid and alone in the cemetery. All the happinesses that appear outside that zone of pain are outbursts of evil.

My Anuarí; my whole body becomes numb at the sole memory of your eternal absence.

XV

I am ill. My hand, burning, slips into a sad faint on the books where I take refuge, to daze myself and forget.

I do not try to open them, it's useless: I can predict them. What can they tell me that takes my thoughts away from your memory? They would only manage to leave a black stain of ink on my pupils luminous from your image. My pain becomes agonizing; my sadness is torn to pieces like the tunics of the martyrs ripped apart by the beasts of the circus.

My temples are heavy as if the fingers of a colossus were pressing into them, and like ceramic urns my eyelids fall.

Anuarí, Anuarí!

Sorrows make my blood heavy, as if cold lava was circulating through my veins.

I am ill. Around me life sings, impious, cruel, with the unconsciousness of an eternally young and joyful goddess.

That chaotic racket makes me think of the desecration of corpses by an inebriated acrobat.

The vibration of pain has destroyed the divine orchestration, which in lyrical union with all my intimate strings, enlivened the celebrations of my soul.

I am so sad, like a dove that the storm surprises, alone and away from its nest.

XVI

Anuarí...

Today I brought you a bouquet of immaculate peonies. When I laid them on your coffin, it seemed to me that the sky had rained stars upon it, and then a delirium of beauty took hold of me.

I wanted to join my lips with those white petals, and for the heaven of my soul to rain kisses, infinite kisses of undreamed-of love upon your body. The sweetness of the tomb penetrated into my brain, like a bath of roses, refreshing it from its passionate yearnings.

My flesh is purified by the white chasteness of the ashes of all the ancestors who rest by your side.

Anuarí; my precious one.

If my sadness were always so gentle that it translated into kisses and flowers, I would bless the pain with the fervor of an enlightened one; I would seek it as the most nourishing spiritual food.

Anuarí: the pain of having lost you is the only human tie that unites us forever.

I love you, and I say so in the flowers that I scatter over you, and in my sobs, which are vigorous like the ebbing of the sea.

From life to your tomb, from your tomb to life, that is my fate.

XVII

Anuarí, my darling.

All the happiness of my days was in your coffin, where I went to lay my head and scatter my flowers.

In my immense loneliness, that was a sweet occupation.

My precious one, I felt you, and in my mad tenderness, I thought no one but me had a right to your corpse.

It was like a blow of iron to the head when I entered the grave and saw you were not in the usual bed.

And when, looking for you like a lioness looks for her lair, I found you in a narrow niche, my pain was as terrible as if you had died a second time.

What cold I felt! And how I felt in my body the martyrdom of your limbs, squeezed together in that narrow prison of stone!

There I will not be able to bring you my flowers; I will not be able to communicate to you the sensation of spring, refreshing your casket with petals, kisses and tears.

XVIII

Anuarí; my sweet precious one, who blows the black sail of my existence toward the paradise of dreams.

Serious angel of the eternal gesture, may you show me, with an exalted sign, the luminous path to the Infinite.

That your coffin has been removed from the reach of my lips produces in me the same terrible desperation that damages the heart of a mother, whom they pull away from the cradle where a child died.

Anuarí, my darling.

I came back from the cemetery suffocated by tears; my tears ran down my chest, soaking it like the beads of an endless necklace.

Here in my bed, where I write, six of your portraits accompany me; to each of them I speak, as if they could hear me.

A humble Christ of steel sits beside me, and I make that sublime man witness to my sorrow.

He died to redeem the world, and I agonize from an impossible love.

We are siblings, we are united in the only noble causes of life; now we hold one another in an intimate embrace, mutually binding ourselves to the only truth: death. Christ and I blend together in the impossible.

I feel in my hands the full weight of my head, as if the life of all human beings were concentrated in it.

It seems like a world held up by two blocks of marble: it seems like a star undergoing internal catastrophe.

Now my hands will no longer scatter petals over your body, and my tears, which were dew, will flood like turbulent waterfalls to destroy the sad but noble ruins, which were the castles of my soul.

XIX

I woke with a start. The clock struck two, and those two severe peals fell on my head like the announcement of the final judgment.

As a dead person rises from the tomb I rose from bed, pushed by a superior force. Disturbed by mystery, without knowing what or where I was, I wanted to flee, and in mad anxiety I stumbled in the darkness over a body, which fell with a sharp thud.

With my hands stretched out like the feelers of a maggot, I searched in the midst of the shadows for something to show me a direction; and my eyes, disproportionately wide open, tried to pierce the night.

My feet did not move, fixed as they were on the ground like two pillars of bronze; a frozen rain soaked my face, dripping fatal liquid onto my temples.

Terrified, trembling, not finding an exit from the labyrinth of my soul, I wanted to succumb. At that moment a beauty from my childhood wounded my memory, and just as I did then, I fell to my knees. On my lips there bloomed a prayer; a deep prayer to my God Anuarí.

With my eyelids shut and my arms raised high, in mystical devotion, my soul begged the heavens to give me the longed-for repose.

Many hours passed, so many that the living tones of dawn wrapped my balcony in pink. That light of life made me consider the reality of events, and only then did I realize that I had passed the whole night in delirious ecstasy before your portrait.

With a smile, the kind which by its placidity seems to be inspired by the stars, I went back to my bed, bearing in my arms the adored relic. I slept, and felt blessed. I dreamed that I was dead and that I was like you, an ideal and good shade.

Anuarí, you are happy because you give to a soul the two sensations of most intense beauty: pain and death.

Anuarí, Anuarí. If I possessed a scythe like the one held by death, I would make use of it to cut off the heads of all the flowers in the world, and lay them as a humble homage on the stone that conceals you.

XX

With a sleepwalker's step I arrive at my desk every night.

Your portrait is there too, spreading over all things a faint reflection of love.

How many times have I wrung out on these pages even the essence of my spirit, and afterward waited, in languid exhaustion, head in hands, for the distant call of your voice, your adored voice, coming from a hazy beyond, forbidden to the souls that still inhabit mortal bodies . . .

Anuarí; I live dreaming of you, vibrating alone with the tremendous caresses that you come to lavish upon me while I sleep; delights that exhaust the cells of my brain.

Upon waking I retain the weight of your body, which rested on my heart; and on my lips the cool graze of your hot mouth.

My ear treasures, like a snatch of music, the penetrating rhythm of your voice.

Anuarí; do you remember those long winter nights without a stove, when to deceive the cold you took my hands firmly, and told me fantastic stories of souls in Purgatory, and we came to be afraid even of the wind that shook the windows?

How happy we were then, and how life seemed to us an easy and pure amusement, like the games of children!

And now that you have gone, what a tragic and fierce cast my life has taken on!

How I have sunk into those sad things, which only belong to the very old!

I am an old woman in the body of a girl, Anuarí. My twenty-four years drag me under, like I am being crushed by a pile of logs. All I can do is raise my eyes to the heavens every so often to assure myself that there, in the infinite, are your two hands, stretched toward me and open like two wings.

XXI

Anuarí, Anuarí! My mouth cannot call you anymore, without a desolate sob cutting off my voice.

Anuarí, my sighs are like those winds that hasten the meeting of the clouds; they are those waves that swell up as they come near the beach, to crash with violence, wrapping the haughty rocks in foam.

Anuarí. An unleashed storm rumbles within my being.

I reveal myself to life; I insult wretched destiny, which has torn all my budding loves from me before I have had a chance to savor their fragrance, or grow intoxicated by their sublime narcotic.

My eyes, wide open, look at the black horizon. I am frightened at the threshold of my life, with a great question stifled on my lips by the horror of the catastrophe.

XXII

Anuarí. Men would judge me crazy if they saw me wandering through the cemeteries like a solitary jackal, which by the awful whims of fate has received a velvet soul.

Anuarí. I search in my empty skull for what I have come to be, and at times feel a vertigo of hastening events and a desire for my thoughts to sleep in the ossuary of oblivion. Anuarí; I want to unite myself with your substance fermented by the vegetable and animal life of nature, to convert myself like you into a universal mass, a marvelous clay from which future geniuses are modeled.

Anuarí. To arrive to you I would suffer the transformation into grass, bird, animal, sea, cloud, ether and, finally, thought. To arrive to you I would unite myself to the secret force that inflames the winds, and would cross the infinite like a meteor, even if it were only to brush against you, like those celestial bodies brush the surface of the sky.

Anuarí, Anuarí; sweetness who captivates my brain in distant ideals. Like light, I have been able to penetrate into nature, to divine its smallest gestures during this time of immense loneliness and pain.

And how I pardon men all their sins and weaknesses!

XXIII

Like the souls that inhabit the cloisters veiled in white or black tulles, my soul changes its clothes in its confidences with life and secret plots with death.

Anuarí. I always prefer the eternal chaos of truth to the rosy illusion of life. The one brings me to you, the other separates me with its infernal seductions, to immediately sink me into the mud of despicable pleasures.

For three months I have lived imprisoned in your memory; and my soul has become so light that it can hold itself in the air like blueness. Anuarí; men pull me from your side with promises of sweetness and beauty, they tempt me as Lucifer tempted the Christ of the Mountain. Many times I have followed them to forget a little of the terrible sorrow of your departure; but it would have been better to have died at your feet, mutilated by pain; it would have been better to have seen with my own eyes the rotting of my flesh, healthily eaten into by dark creatures. Anuarí; does the disgrace of the world have no limits? Is pain so unbearable that the good become bad and the bad perverse? Pain sanctifies sublime souls and drags down inferior ones . . . there is no doubt, Anuarí.

XXIV

Wandering through lonely forests alongside stagnant pools, I have thought of all the sadness in those souls, born of a ray of sun or moon, that look around to find themselves orphaned.

I understand the vice of love, that in a spasm of pleasure makes us believe in nobility; I understand that in the kiss and surrender of bodies one seeks the poison of oblivion; because that makes man a god and woman a sacred vase, a depositary urn for sap, which is the life of creation.

Anuarí; I understand that once the loved god is dead, the insides of the beloved shatter with the pain of not having received those sweet diluted pearls, and remain sad and lonely as antique amphoras, crying out at the neglect of their owner.

XXV

Today I brought jasmines for you.

White flowers of piercing fragrance which, like white butterflies, fell asleep on the stone.

It was raining. The water sang shyly on the memorials and gravestones of the cemetery, trickling through the hollows of the tombs, anxious to refresh the mouths of the dead.

Black clouds, heavy with divine power, burst open noisily in the loneliness of the sky.

My head, not conscious of life, happily received the caress of rain, and like a bird content with its bath, remained unmoving under the affectionate dripping of warm drops. You were there, at the height of my forehead. My hands, resting on your coffin, had an ecstatic stillness, like the hands of Indian idols who retain the delicious secret of tranquility as they think of Nirvana.

You were there, sheltered from the rain in your little marble house; and asleep, asleep like a boy who has played a long time and is tired. Anuarí, my darling. Your abode is very narrow. Won't you make a little place where your little sister can shelter herself too?

But the sleeping are very egoistic, they do not remember the poor mendicants who remain under the windows, with no coat but sorrow.

When it grew dark and I heard the bell that announced the close of the cemetery gates, I said goodbye to you, just as I did that August night, do you remember? when we kissed twenty times, saying goodbye to one another, and twenty times returned to embrace without being able to separate.

Oh, Anuarí! How is it that my heart does not burst in a storm like that of the sky, when it is so overshadowed by pain?

XXVI

The ice that melts insistently through the torn places in my windows makes me shiver.

How deeply I think of you, and your gentle kisses; and I long for the warmth of your body clinging tightly against mine, like a ribbon of skin!

You were my dear one; the little soft and golden sunbeam that came to cheer up the gloomy cavern where my skepticism lives like a wild beast.

How I felt myself yours!

Did you know the dense veils my soul crossed through to wrap you in a luminous caress, to contemplate you anointed with purity? Anuarí. The bed, the pillow, even the window seem to retain your silhouette.

Wherever I look you are there, and when I breathe, it is your smell that penetrates me; I speak, and the echo of my words seems like an imitation of your voice.

Your kisses, when you sowed them on my lips, made my mouth a field of wheat, and now, in your eternal absence, those grains have become flowers of adoration; and the caresses you left on my body are brilliant engravings full of shadows and the paleness of pearl that cannot animate life.

Anuarí, I am everything in you; as you are everything in me.

XXVII

Before my eyes is the face of your portrait; I lean forward, heavy with inspiration. I look with my heart overflowing with deep tenderness.

Little bird of mine: why did you go?

If I knew how to love you, more than anyone you could find in paradise.

If I could become intoxicated on your essence, more than a bird intoxicated on flowers.

Why did you give me the liquor of life to drink from your lips, if you would have to abandon me still thirsty?

Like a lamp without oil I consume myself, feeling all the agonies of sorrow.

The bracelets that adorn my arms sound like the clapper of a dead bell, and with a resounding collapse the marble tower of my daydreams falls, where I saw the sky: where I saw you.

My eyes, my mouth, my arms that shift about like logs caressed by the fire, are full of tenderness. But you will not come; and like a tree tired of waiting for the touch of the moon, I will bend forward my sorrowing face.

XXVIII

Alone, amidst my papers and books, your beloved memory visits me, all dressed in white.

Your hands, which when they caressed mine were so good, now from a distance and with an eternal gesture cause me pain.

The aristocratic beauty of your hands makes me hate all the others stretched toward me.

I want only your white ones, yours that were lilies sick with sadness.

And I want your eyes that lingered fraternally in the midst of the passionate hurricane of our caresses . . .

And your mouth, which always had that grimace of a wise boy who has an intuition about everything, without having experienced anything . . .

And your bending body clinging to mine in the eagerness for death, and for life . . .

And your soul, a sacred pitcher that put out the fire of my anxieties and idealisms, putting me to sleep in an ecstasy of sublime drowsiness . . .

Yes; your hands, your eyes, your mouth, your body and your soul; yes, all mine, I call to you, I love you, I love you . . . You have gone, little bird of mine. You have gone, but your sweet distress remains, caressing my ear.

If it had been possible to die of happy languor, I would have died last night, when in dreams you came to rest your cheek alongside mine.

You were gentle, Anuarí. But your pale face, with its childish innocence, retained its image on my retina, caressing my interior.

The tragic secret of silence guards you like a great wall of rock, but I will come to you. My sorrow will transform me into a specter so delicate that I will pass through the stone. Anuarí, I am waiting for you.

XXIX

I have turned off all the lights, leaving an oil lamp lit in the middle of the living room at night, like the one that guards the Almighty in the temple, and that spreads mystic tenderness.

The bell of the tower has struck twelve, and I still cannot make out the sound of your spirit when it comes to visit me; I still cannot hear the murmur of your voice by my ear, nor feel the brush of your hand on my submissive chin.

I tremble, afraid that you will not come, and that all my longings will die in painful despair on my pillow. I tremble, Anuarí, my love, my tender one . . .

When I evoke you, there is such purity in my feeling that I am like a white lily; and my soul becomes a dove that still has not rehearsed its first flight.

Won't you come?

I let my head fall on the hand of mine which you kissed so much, and the sadness of the world seems deeper and life more difficult to bear.

Anuarí! you will not come, you will not come; my pessimism tells me, that voice tells me which foretold to me our departure and the departure of all I have most loved.

You will not come; and now I do not expect the coolness of your intangible hands on my forehead, and I shiver with anxiety. Will my prayers be useless, useless the deliriums of my love?

Save me, save me from life, from the terror of myself, from spiritual misery!

Save me, pull me away from the earth before an evil shadow wraps itself around me and sweeps me toward the infernal chaos of oblivion and resignation.

XXX

Anuarí. I look at my lips in the mirror and I curse. By what strange irony are they so red? Why, if you, the one who inflamed them, has gone? They should go pale with love, like my heart, and like my hands, which have become mystical flowers from so much imploring death. To whom can I offer my bloody lips, without giving to him, like the poison of a serpent, the fatal narcotic of my sadness?

No longer will you come to ask kisses of me.

I look at my bright eyes, like children of the sun, and close them, frightened. I do not want their beauty . . . if you do not come to see yourself in them.

You, who were their light, have extinguished yourself like a will-o'-the-wisp in the waves of the sea.

Anuarí, my idol.

I contemplate my youth like an open rose, and scorn the morbidity that offers itself, pagan, provocative, shameless, defying my pain which hides itself, anguished and shy.

No; no longer will you come to pull from my body the lyric and vibrant note of the spasm, the choked sob of pleasure.

Anaurí, Anuarí! Fullness of my soul, emotion and feeling, reason for my existence!

Will you be able to understand the awful mutilation of my being at your going so abruptly, for eternity?

I will make you the sacrifice of my youth like a nun to her God, and it will be the best offering of love that I can make to your memory.

Anuarí . . .

XXXI

You came to me; I did not expect you. I was not expecting happiness.

I had lost everything, and I found everything when you stretched your arms toward me.

'Take me,' I said. I will be faithful to your heart, and with enchanting gentleness it will heal the profound wounds of mine. I will live through you; the brilliance of your eyes will be my light, to hide myself trustingly in your chest will be my joy; I will laugh when I see your lips separate, from internal ecstasy; I will cry when you cry, and will love you, deliciously gratified by your tenderness; I will love you with all the fire of the eternal lover.

XXXII

My life is yours, because you saved it for yourself.

You invited me to mingle myself with the great symphony of Nature, and when my soul had already begun to desire the sun again, you left like a wandering shade toward treacherous night.

Anuarí, the divine prayer of love came to beat against my heart as gently as the flapping of wings . . .

I loved love with the passion of a frenzied woman, and clung to it, because for such a long time I ran devastated in search of you.

XXXIII

Anuarí, Anuarí, why did you go?

My hands twist; my lips curse, and my eyes grow fixed, fixed like those perverse stars that destroy the destiny of men. The dark beauty of lyrical evil stretches harmonious veils over my face, which lower over my body and wrap it like a pliant sea algae.

It is the evil of sorrow, of black sorrow.

Anuarí . . .

Before your gravestone my heart no longer cries, it grows cold as marble.

My flowers die burnt up by the sun, like little old ladies who have suffered greatly. Only my head is tortured when it leans over the stone, searching anxiously for the cold embrace.

Each day that passes is a drop that pierces into the subterranean room of my pain.

A flickering flame, my spirit is tossed about like a toy in the macabre wind, which whistles threateningly, destructively, in the abandoned hollows of my mind.

I no longer know how to live, yet I live; nor do I know how to die, for I lack the strength to close my eyes.

XXXIV

I move away . . .

My only despair is that I cannot bring flowers with my own hands to the miserly tomb that keeps you.

Before going I will stamp a kiss on your rigid forehead. It will be like a seal of stone on another stone.

I go, fleeing from myself, from my cowardice and my anxieties.

I cannot die of pain, and the moral torture that stirs my brain is stronger than death itself.

I go like a meteorite emitted from a star that rushes through the tragic spaces of blood.

I go, to learn by other sufferings to suffer mine with greater strength. I go, Anuarí, and I swear to you that to this moment I have been waiting for resurrection. I have been watching your dream, believing it to be a light one, and I flee now that I know it to be marble, Anuarí. The world does not matter to me, nor the mediocre balance that weighs my acts; few are the souls who have loved, enjoyed and suffered as I have.

XXXV

Anuarí. Goodbye for now. From here my thoughts will offer themselves to you as you cross the seas; from here I will watch over your remains with the most vast and fervent memory.

Soon we will find one another, my darling.

My head is an abyss of pain where my thoughts roll about without stop, like agile stones.

I try to think and my reflections fall and roll like dark beads off the cliff of nothingness.

There exists only one truth as great as the sun: death.

Writing to the Dead: On Teresa Wilms Montt's *In the Stillness of Marble*

Buenos Aires, 1917. Twenty-two-year-old poet Horacio Ramos Mejía kills himself in front of Chilean writer Teresa Wilms Montt, desperate to escape the pains of his unreciprocated love. In response to this traumatic event, Wilms Montt moves to Madrid and the following year publishes *En la quietud del mármol* (*In the Stillness of Marble*), a set of thirty-five prose poems that directly address the dead poet. This is not her first work, but it moves the coy language of her two previous books into tragic, more personal territory. The poems are intimate; they read not as letters, but rather as prayers or incantations:

> And when the sun spills out diamonds upon the world, then I breathe in all the flowers, I see you in all the trees, and I possess you tumbling, intoxicated with love, on the lawns of fragrant grass.
> And when the moon gives its humble blessing to men, I see you gigantic, silhouetted by the sharp edges of a lightning bolt; I see you enormous, confused with the immortal, scattering your indulgence over the world, soothing the desperation of so many suffering castaways; I breathe you in the atmosphere, I imagine you in the mystery, I extract you from nothingness.
> It seems to me that the world was only made to help me evoke you, and the sun to serve me as a lantern over the rugged path.

In the Stillness of Marble responds to death, incorporating Catholic, pagan, and personal influences to trace a trajectory from sorrow to acceptance. At its primary level it is a record of grief, but it is also self-conscious about the beauty that can be found in this grief, and the immortalization of the writer through her depiction of it. An ambiguity hovers in Wilms Montt's poems between longings for the dead and reminders that he now lives on through her work, a trope used in turn to ironically assert the importance of a carpe diem approach, given the brevity of life, and the importance of these love notes, given that they are what will survive the vast deserts of eternity.

Wilms Montt reworked these familiar oppositions of metaphysical poetry by casting herself in the role of the poet attentive to death yet avid for life. Her intimate approach and sensuality set her apart even from other Chilean poets of the time, who were also interested in themes of death and the beauty that lingers. Writing at a particularly fertile period in Chilean poetic history, Wilms Montt's contemporaries included Pedro Prado (*Los pájaros errantes* [The Wandering Birds], 1915) and the group Los Diez, Gabriela Mistral (*Sonetos de la muerte* [Sonnets of Death], 1914), and Vicente Huidobro (*Las pagodas ocultas* [The Hidden Pagodas], 1916), the last of whom would for a time be her companion.

Wilms Montt was born on September 8, 1893 in Viña del Mar, Chile, into an elite, well-connected family. She was brought up by governesses who taught her all the techniques for finding a good husband, studied languages, piano and singing, and attended many luxurious banquets. From a young age, however, she showed a creative spirit that rebelled against the norms of her class. At an event at her father's house in the summer of 1910, she met Gustavo Balmaceda Valdés, a direct relative of the ex-president José Manuel Balmaceda. He was eight years older than her and worked for the internal revenue service. Despite opposition from both families, the seventeen-year-old Wilms Montt joined Balmaceda in marriage, and they had two daughters.

Wilms Montt's restlessness and her husband's jealousy, though, were problematic for the couple. Between 1911 and 1914 the family moved from city to city, as far apart as Valdivia and Iquique. These years of solitude were creatively productive for Wilms Montt. She worked on her private diaries and developed close friendships with many influential artists and intellectuals, such as the poet Víctor Domingo Silva. In Iquique, she published her writing under the pseudonym 'Tebac' and began to develop ideals inspired by the Spanish feminist Belén de Zárraga and the Chilean revolutionary leftist Luis Emilio Recabarren. Noting this change, Gustavo Balmaceda sent her back to Santiago, where she remained under the care of her paternal family. Months later, she was forced into a nunnery, the Convent of Precious Blood. In 1916, after a suicide attempt, she escaped to Buenos Aires with the help of her then-lover Huidobro.

Arrival in the city led her to embrace her autonomy as a woman and writer. She began to collaborate with the magazine *Nosotros*, which also published work by Gabriela Mistral and Ángel Cruchaga Santa María. In 1917, she published her first two books. The first, *Inquietudes sentimentales* (Sentimental Doubts), consisted of fifty poems with surrealist features, while her second work, *Los tres cantos* (Three Songs), explored eroticism and spirituality. Both books enjoyed great success in Argentine intellectual circles. In 1918, Wilms Montt moved to Madrid. There she published two works widely recognized by Spanish literary critics: *In the Stillness of Marble* and *Anuarí*.

When Wilms Montt returned to Buenos Aires in 1919, she published her fifth book, titled *Cuentos para hombres que todavía son niños* (Stories for Men who Remain Boys), in which she evokes her childhood and some intimate experiences in a fantastic key. She continued to travel across Europe, visiting London and Paris, but maintaining her residence in Madrid. In 1920, she reunited with her children in Paris, but after their departure, she grew gravely ill. During this crisis, she consumed a high dose of Veronal and, after a long period of agony, died on December 24, 1921. She was twenty-eight years old.

Why does one speak to the dead? The dead cannot talk back; they can only listen. Perhaps there is something about the act of writing to the dead, just as there is in praying, something sacred that is not simple consolation but an opening of oneself to new possibilities. Wilms Montt's text might be read as a familiar psychological journey, almost adhering to the Kübler-Ross model: grief of the loss of a loved one, transmutation of the dead person into a symbol, and renewed attention to self. Of course these three stages are undergone in Wilms Montt's own key of anguish and irony, and experienced as writing. Widely experienced as the events of love and death are, here they are created afresh.

Grieving comes first. Before reading Wilms Montt, one might imagine that she writes to purge herself of horror and perhaps culpability. After all, a man shot himself in front of her out of despair because she did not return his love. Yet notably, while the text expresses disbelief and sorrow, as well as feelings of resentment, longing, desire, and loneliness, there is never guilt. Wilms Montt accompanied her 'Anuarí' (an invented nickname) in a sensual way, and this is also how she misses him. Her descriptions are curiously unsentimental, despite their claims to the contrary. The most heartfelt phrases are brutal declarations of eroticism, such as 'My mouth is thirsty with lust' and 'I came to your niche, to your narrow and wretched cavern, with the desire to turn myself to velvet, to bundle you up, to wrap you in myself, to give you an impression of love.' Wilms Montt portrays herself as alone in this luxurious grieving, this frantic distress. She even hints that she is judged for such extended unhappiness. This setup creates an inversion, as if she herself is now the victim, the one to be pitied.

At some point, a transmutation takes place: the living person is abstracted. The word 'Anuarí' is a fiction, and as an invocation reiterated a full sixty times within the text, its presence displaces the initial direct address to the dead man, transforming him into an emblem. This is the first step of both art and acceptance. The concept of *Amor* is idealized beyond the person of Anuarí, even if the dead man's name calls it to mind. The dead one becomes an almost pagan idol, his memory worshipped as a god in place of the living person. In a provocative section, Wilms Montt falls asleep with photos of Anuarí and a steel statue of Christ. 'We are siblings, we are united in the only noble causes of life; now we hold one another in an intimate embrace, mutually binding ourselves to the only truth: death. Christ and I blend together in the impossible,' she writes. Anuarí has become a symbol of sorrow and longed-for resurrection, and it is this transmutation which makes possible such profane mystical identification with Christ.

Reading *In the Stillness of Marble*, the real tragedy seems to be not death itself—for in death one is close to God and the beyond, all enigmas are revealed, and peace reigns—but rather the fact that Wilms Montt has not died as well. What she expresses is jealousy of the dead, and a desire to perish:

> Anuarí. To arrive to you I would suffer the transformation into grass, bird, animal, sea, cloud, ether and, finally, thought. To arrive to you I would unite myself to the secret force that inflames the winds, and would cross the infinite like a meteor, even if it were only to brush against you, like those celestial bodies brush the surface of the sky.

In her early text *Iniciación* (Initiation), part of the diaries she kept but did not publish in her lifetime, Wilms Montt refers to herself from the position of a dead person, which she describes as a pleasant dream or blissful oblivion. This text is autobiographical, and in it she describes herself in the third person in language remarkably similar to that of *In the Stillness of Marble*.

To dream without cease, enclosed within the walls of marble, smooth and clean, of a tomb; to dream for all eternity. She will remain still, with the rigidity of dolls, and her soul will breathe in the perfume of her favorite flowers, the flowers with which her sisters will have crowned her head. The peace of death will climb slowly up her feet, to arrive silent as the tide . . . She will be wrapped in the serenity of velvet . . . Then she will discover the secret of that voice that murmurs enigmas to her heart . . . that voice that comes from beyond life.

Death itself, the condition of death, does not frighten her. She concludes, 'To die must be something like sinking into a warm bath during frozen nights.'

Wilms Montt's earlier and later works, sadly separated by only a few years, are continuous in form. The fragmentation of *In the Stillness of Marble* is similar to that of Wilms Montt's previous writing in her diary, especially those parts recorded when she was in the Chilean nunnery. Of the diary, literary critic Ruth González-Vergara writes that it is 'at once a ludic form of exercising memory and of looking back on pleasant moments as a palliative to the stigma of being prisoner. There are flashes of irony and humor, not free of sensuality, that at times develop into a certain frivolity despite the sacredness and severity of the atmosphere.'

As with the nunnery, the cemetery. Despite the gravity of the situation, *In the Stillness of Marble* avoids solemnity in large part due to its own self-awareness in the acting-out of grief. As the dead man finds rest as representation, we enter the final stage, in which Wilms Montt herself becomes the poem's focus. The book arcs from Wilms Montt's distress to her consciousness of the consequences of this distress. She alludes to attentions from other men. Her own beauty is repeatedly evoked. Grief takes on a theatrical quality, a vanity that both fascinates and troubles. Her red lips, her forehead, even her cold body draped over the tomb assume a certain seduction. Once again, Wilms Montt enters unexplored and uncomfortable territory. What is the seductive quality of grief? Here the living erotic body is continuously juxtaposed with the still corpse, to make the reader feel not only that the writer's grief is absurd in its intensity and longevity, but also that the poet ought to accept the invitations of the healthy young life around her.

The insinuation is that Wilms Montt's own existence has come to a halt; it, too, is still as marble. If she continues to grieve, she will herself become dead in life—an escalation of the tragedy. She must move on. The balance between personal feeling, duty to oneself, and societal expectation is delicate. Wilms Montt's own beauty takes on a special importance, used as an apologia and an escape hatch from the drudgery of grieving. The deeply romantic idea here is that beauty is above moral constraints. Beauty can be cruel; for beauty, anything is possible. The prologue by Guatemalan journalist Enrique Gómez Carillo, an infamous dandy, props up this idea with his slavish declarations of admiration, referencing Wilms Montt's 'curse of beauty'.

Wilms Montt's book, *Anuarí*, was published in Madrid the same year as *In the Stillness of Marble*, with a prologue by the Spanish writer Ramón del Valle-Inclán. The text of *Anuarí* is different from that of *In the Stillness of Marble*, even if the style and theme are similar, and the two can be read as companion pieces. Precisely because of this similarity, however, there is some confusion. In the introduction by González-Vergara to the 1994 version of the complete works, *Anuarí* is listed as a disappeared edition, and we read that: 'The book of poems *Anuarí* has been impossible to find in Chile, Argentina, Spain, France, and the United States, for which reason it does not appear in the present edition. Verifiable news about its existence allows one to harbor future hopes. Part of the prologue by Valle-Inclán is known.' In the edition of the collected works of Wilms Montt called *Lo que no se ha dicho* (What Has Not Been Said), released by Editorial Nascimento in 1922, a text called *Anuarí* does appear, but the poems correspond to those of *In the Stillness of Marble*; two poems have also been combined into one. Unfortunately, this book remains the one on the Memoria Chilena page for Wilms Montt's work, which has resulted in re-editions that replicate the error. In 2016 this confusion was clarified when the Chilean editor Alquimia used an edition printed in Madrid to publish the correct version of *Anuarí*. Like other works of hers, it was originally signed with the pseudonym Thérèse de la †.

The ghostly rewriting of *In the Stillness of Marble* in the form of a second text, so similar that it has misled even academics of her work, suggests that the theme transformed into an *idée fixe* for Wilms Montt, one that she did not feel she could exhaust in a single book. The spirit of Anuarí continued to haunt her.

A poem with 'marble' in its name suggests eternity, and *In the Stillness of Marble* is a fixing of the sensuous movements of life into timelessness. The cool hard substance is the materialization of the immortal, and its universal presence in majestic buildings from the Taj Mahal to the Palace of Versailles haunts Anuarí's tomb like a holy spirit every time Wilms Montt presses her head and lips against it. She has transformed the tomb she caresses into an architectural monument. The stillness of marble could have multiple interpretations—the Immobility of a Dead Beloved, the Immortalized State of Poetry, the Impasse of One's Life. For Wilms Montt it refers to all three—the eternity of her lover, the memorial of this book, and the standstill of her own life, which she must overcome.

In the Stillness of Marble is a work that explores quietude, yet uses its own lyrical propulsion to generate kinetic motion. To write to the dead is a process of self-invention, self-affirmation. It is a way of defining oneself in contrast to stillness, as a living being; it is a way of affirming existence through negation, with a greater complexity than simple acceptance. Wilms Montt romanticizes death as she does beauty, as a stillness to be admired, an occult face concealing secrets. At the same time, her own prose poetry makes it clear that life with its heat and movement is also to be admired. The contradiction here, and in the attitude of Wilms Montt, is what gives this work such vibrance: *quietud* is engaged in a vital tangle with *inquietud*.

Jessica Sequeira

A PARTIAL LIST OF SNUGGLY BOOKS

LÉON BLOY *The Tarantulas' Parlor and Other Unkind Tales*
S. HENRY BERTHOUD *Misanthropic Tales*
FÉLICIEN CHAMPSAUR *The Latin Orgy*
FÉLICIEN CHAMPSAUR
  The Emerald Princess and Other Decadent Fantasies
BRENDAN CONNELL *Clark*
BRENDAN CONNELL *Jottings from a Far Away Place*
BRENDAN CONNELL *Unofficial History of Pi Wei*
ADOLFO COUVE *When I Think of My Missing Head*
QUENTIN S. CRISP *Aiaigasa*
QUENTIN S. CRISP *Blue on Blue*
QUENTIN S. CRISP *Rule Dementia!*
LADY DILKE *The Outcast Spirit and Other Stories*
BERIT ELLINGSEN *Now We Can See the Moon*
BERIT ELLINGSEN *Vessel and Solsvart*
EDMOND AND JULES DE GONCOURT *Manette Salomon*
RHYS HUGHES *Cloud Farming in Wales*
COLIN INSOLE *Valerie and Other Stories*
JUSTIN ISIS *Pleasant Tales II*
JUSTIN ISIS (editor) *Marked to Die: A Tribute to Mark Samuels*
JUSTIN ISIS AND DANIEL CORRICK (editors)
  Drowning in Beauty: The Neo-Decadent Anthology
VICTOR JOLY *The Unknown Collaborator and Other Legendary Tales*
BERNARD LAZARE *The Mirror of Legends*
BERNARD LAZARE *The Torch-Bearers*
JEAN LORRAIN *Errant Vice*
JEAN LORRAIN *Masks in the Tapestry*
JEAN LORRAIN *Nightmares of an Ether-Drinker*
JEAN LORRAIN *The Soul-Drinker and Other Decadent Fantasies*

ARTHUR MACHEN *N*
ARTHUR MACHEN *Ornaments in Jade*
CAMILLE MAUCLAIR *The Frail Soul and Other Stories*
CATULLE MENDÈS *Bluebirds*
CATULLE MENDÈS *Mephistophela*
LUIS DE MIRANDA *Who Killed the Poet?*
OCTAVE MIRBEAU *The Death of Balzac*
CHARLES MORICE *Babels, Balloons and Innocent Eyes*
DAMIAN MURPHY *Daughters of Apostasy*
DAMIAN MURPHY *The Star of Gnosia*
KRISTINE ONG MUSLIM *Butterfly Dream*
YARROW PAISLEY *Mendicant City*
URSULA PFLUG *Down From*
JEAN RICHEPIN *The Bull-Man and the Grasshopper*
DAVID RIX *A Suite in Four Windows*
FREDERICK ROLFE (Baron Corvo)
  An Ossuary of the North Lagoon and Other Stories
JASON ROLFE *An Archive of Human Nonsense*
BRIAN STABLEFORD *Spirits of the Vasty Deep*
BRIAN STABLEFORD (editor)
  Decadence and Symbolism: A Showcase Anthology
TOADHOUSE *Gone Fishing with Samy Rosenstock*
JANE DE LA VAUDÈRE *The Demi-Sexes and The Androgynes*
JANE DE LA VAUDÈRE *The Double Star and Other Occult Fantasies*
JANE DE LA VAUDÈRE *The Mystery of Kama and Brahma's Courtesan*
JANE DE LA VAUDÈRE *Syta's Harem and Pharaoh's Lover*
JANE DE LA VAUDÈRE *Three Flowers and the King of Siam's Amazon*
JANE DE LA VAUDÈRE *The Witch of Ecbatana and the Virgin of Israel*
RENÉE VIVIEN *Lilith's Legacy*
RENÉE VIVIEN *A Woman Appeared to Me*
RENÉE VIVIEN AND HÉLÈNE DE ZUYLEN DE NYEVELT
  Faustina and Other Stories

www.ingramcontent.com/pod-product-compliance
Lightning Source LLC
Chambersburg PA
CBHW020125130526
44591CB00032B/537